SandCastle™

Let's Measure More

WHAT IN THE WORLD IS A MILE?

AND OTHER DISTANCE MEASUREMENTS

A Division of ABDO

ABDO
Publishing Company

Desirée Bussiere

Consulting Editor, Diane Craig, M.A./Reading Specialist

visit us at www.abdopublishing.com

Published by ABDO Publishing Company, a division of ABDO, P.O. Box 398166, Minneapolis, Minnesota 55439. Copyright © 2013 by Abdo Consulting Group, Inc. International copyrights reserved in all countries. No part of this book may be reproduced in any form without written permission from the publisher. SandCastle™ is a trademark and logo of ABDO Publishing Company.

Printed in the United States of America, North Mankato, Minnesota
102012
012013

 PRINTED ON RECYCLED PAPER

Editor: Liz Salzmann
Content Developer: Nancy Tuminelly
Cover and Interior Design: Colleen Dolphin, Mighty Media, Inc.
Cover and Interior Production: Kate Hartman
Photo Credits: Shutterstock

Library of Congress Cataloging-in-Publication Data

Bussierre, Desireé, 1989-
  What in the world is a mile? : and other distance measurements / Desireé Bussierre ; consulting editor, Diane Craig, M.A./reading specialist.
      pages cm. -- (Let's measure more)
  Audience: 4-9
  ISBN 978-1-61783-598-8
  1. Length measurement--Juvenile literature. 2. Distances--Measurement--Juvenile literature.
  3. Units of measurement--Juvenile literature. I. Title.
  QC102.B87 2013
  530.8'1--dc23
                              2012025985

SandCastle™ Level: Transitional

SandCastle™ books are created by a team of professional educators, reading specialists, and content developers around five essential components—phonemic awareness, phonics, vocabulary, text comprehension, and fluency—to assist young readers as they develop reading skills and strategies and increase their general knowledge. All books are written, reviewed, and leveled for guided reading, early reading intervention, and Accelerated Reader® programs for use in shared, guided, and independent reading and writing activities to support a balanced approach to literacy instruction. The SandCastle™ series has four levels that correspond to early literacy development. The levels are provided to help teachers and parents select appropriate books for young readers.

Emerging Readers
(no flags)

Beginning Readers
(1 flag)

Transitional Readers
(2 flags)

Fluent Readers
(3 flags)

Contents

Distance is the space between two places or things.

Inches, feet, yards, and miles are ways to measure distance.

distance?

What is

An inch is small. Inches are used to measure short distances.

You can measure inches with a ruler.

1 inch

an inch?

Sue measures the distance between her doll and her bear. They are 7 inches apart.

7 inches

A foot is bigger than an inch. There are 12 inches in 1 foot.

1 foot

a foot?

Bob and John have **lockers** near each other. They are 2 feet apart.

A yard is bigger than a foot. There are 3 feet in 1 yard.

A football field is measured in yards. There are 100 yards between the end **zones.**

yard?

Jake plays football. He ran 15 yards in today's game.

Miles are used to measure long distances. There are 5,280 feet in 1 mile.

mile?

Mary's family is taking a long trip. They are going to visit Mary's grandma. She lives in Iowa. That's 475 miles away.

Miles per hour is a way to measure speed. It is the number of miles traveled in one hour.

miles per hour?

Willie's dad drives 60 miles per hour on the **highway.** He drives 30 miles per hour on city streets.

A light-year is the distance light travels in one year. One light-year is almost 6 **trillion** miles!

Scientists use light-years to measure distances in space.

light-year?

Amy is learning about stars. Many stars are thousands of light-years away.

A furlong is an old way to measure distance. It is 220 yards. That was about how long a farmer's field was.

Today the furlong is used in horse racing. Racetracks are often measured in furlongs.

furlong?

Greg loves horses. His grandpa takes him to the races every May. The track is 10 furlongs around.

A league is another old way to measure distance. It is about 3 miles. That is how far a person or horse can walk in 1 hour.

The league is **hardly** ever used today. But you might read about leagues in books.

league?

Sally reads before going to sleep. The people in the story are on a long journey. They travel many leagues.

Fun facts

⇨ The foot was based on the average size of a man's foot. That's how it got its name.

⇨ Sailors use **nautical** miles. The nautical mile is based on the lines on a map. It is a little longer than a regular mile.

⇨ An odometer measures how far something has traveled. Every car and truck has an odometer.

⇨ The word *light-year* was first used by Friedrich Bessel in 1838.

Quiz

Read each sentence below. Then decide whether it is true or false.

(1) Inches are used to measure short distances.
True or False?

(2) One mile equals to 5,280 feet. True or False?

(3) Willie's mom drives 30 miles per hour on the
highway. True or False?

(4) Light-years are used to measure distances in space.
True or False?

(5) Furlongs are used to measure football fields.
True or False?

Answers: 1. True 2. True 3. False 4. True 5. False

Glossary

hardly — rarely or almost never.

highway — a major road, especially one that people use to go from one town to another.

locker — a closet with a lock that a student can put personal things in.

nautical — related to sailors, navigation, or ships.

trillion — a very large number. One trillion is also written 1,000,000,000,000.

zone — an area that is set off for a specific use or purpose.